£12.99

Reflecting On and Developing Your Practice

Knowledge and Skills for Social Care Workers series

The Knowledge and Skills for Social Care Workers series features accessible open learning workbooks which tackle a range of key subjects relevant to people working with adults in residential or domiciliary settings. Not just a source of guidance, these workbooks are also designed to meet the requirements of Health and Social Care (Adults) NVQ Level 3, with interactive exercises to develop practice.

other books in the series

Effective Communication
A Workbook for Social Care Workers
Suzan Collins
ISBN 978 1 84310 927 3

Safeguarding Adults
A Workbook for Social Care Workers
Suzan Collins
ISBN 978 1 84310 928 0

Health and Safety
A Workbook for Social Care Workers
Suzan Collins
ISBN 978 1 84310 929 7

Reflecting On and Developing Your Practice

A Workbook for Social Care Workers

Suzan Collins

Jessica Kingsley Publishers
London and Philadelphia

First published in 2009
by Jessica Kingsley Publishers
116 Pentonville Road
London N1 9JB, UK
and
400 Market Street, Suite 400
Philadelphia, PA 19106, USA

www.jkp.com

Library of Congress Cataloging in Publication Data
A CIP catalog record for this book is available from the Library of Congress

British Library Cataloguing in Publication Data
A CIP catalogue record for this book is available from the British Library

Process of Learning diagram, p.31: all reasonable efforts to trace the copyright holder have been made, and any enquiries should be addressed to the publisher.

ISBN 978 1 84310 930 3

Printed and bound in Great Britain by
Printwise (Haverhill) Ltd, Suffolk

Acknowledgements

Simon Kent (Final year student social worker) for his advice and support

Lee Nevill (Lowestoft College) for his assistance and support

This workbook meets the requirements of the following standards, guidance and qualifications

General Social Care Inspection (CSCI)
Care Home for Adults Standard 36
Domiciliary Care 21

General Social Care Council (GSCC)
Code of Practice Standard 6

Learning Disability Qualification Induction Award
LDQIA Level 3, Unit 302

National Vocational Qualification in Health and Social Care
NVQ HSC Level 3, Unit 33

Skills for Care (SfC)
Common Induction Standard 6

Contents

Introduction

as a social care worker, [you] must be accountable for the quality of [your] work and take responsibility for maintaining and improving [your] knowledge and skills.

(General Social Care Council 2002)

This workbook will provide you with guidance on how you can improve your knowledge and how to reflect on your practice: thinking about what you do, how you do it and why you do it, with the aim of improving your practice.

It is not always possible for staff to be taken off the rota to attend a training course and so this workbook has been devised. It uses a variety of training methods:

- reading passages where you will expand your knowledge

- completing exercises

- completing a self-assessment tool which shows you the knowledge you now have

As a social care worker, you have to work to certain standards, which are set out by various professional bodies. This workbook links to several standards and in case are not familiar with them, here is a brief explanation of each one.

Learning Disability Qualification Induction Award (LDQ_IA) is an induction award that all new staff working with people with learning disabilities must complete within three months of being in post. This workbook meets the requirements of the Level 3 award, Unit 302 Task A.

Skills for Care (SfC) has a set of standards called Common Induction Standards and all new staff in the care sector (except those who are supporting people with learning disabilities) have to complete these with their manager within three months of being in post. This workbook meets the requirements of Standard 6.

Care Quality Commission (CQC) took over the work of the Commission for Social Care Inspection (CSCI) on 1 April 2009 (it also took over the work of the Healthcare Commission and the Mental Health Act Commission). The CQC has sets of standards for you and your workplace to meet. There are different sets of standards and it will depend on where you work as to which standards you need to work too. If you are unsure, please ask your manager.

General Social Care Council (GSCC) has a Code of Practice with six standards in it that reflect good practice. This workbook meets the requirements of Standard 6.

Towards the end of the workbook you will be asked to complete a self-assessment questionnaire on what you have learnt from completing this workbook. Once you have completed this, your manager or trainer will complete the certificate and give it to you.

NVQ HSC is a *National Vocational Qualification in Health and Social Care.* This workbook has been written first and foremost to enable you to improve your knowledge and skills and if you are thinking about doing or working towards an NVQ Level 3 in Health and Social Care, you will find that this workbook is a great help to you.

The Health and Social Care Level 3 has four core units and four optional units. This workbook is one of the four core units written to show the knowledge specification. The other three core units are available in this series of books: *Health and Safety, Safeguarding Adults* and *Effective Communication.*

When you have registered for an NVQ, you will be allocated an NVQ Assessor who will arrange to observe you in the workplace and guide you through your NVQ award. This guidance will involve devising action plans, which will consist of things like:

- Writing an account of how you did something in the workplace, e.g. helping someone to make a cup of tea, or providing support to enable a service user to follow a training programme, identifying risks, supporting someone to go to the shops etc. This is called a 'self-reflective account' (SRA).

- Asking others to write an account of what you have done. This is called a 'witness report' (WR).

- Completing a set of questions which is called 'the knowledge specification'. This is where you can use this workbook for reference.

This workbook covers all the knowledge specification requirements for the NVQ Unit 33 'Reflect on and develop your practice', which can be found towards the end of this workbook (see Knowledge Specification Chart).

I hope that you find this a useful workbook and wish you well in your career. This workbook can be:

- read straight through from front to back

- read from front to back, answering the questions as you go, and these can be used as evidence towards the NVQ Unit 33

- used as a reference book.

In this workbook I have referred to the people you support as 'individuals' 'service users' or 'he/him' rather than continually writing he/she him/her.

Name of Learner: ....

Signature of Learner: .... Date: ....

Name of Manager or Trainer: ....

Signature of Manager or Trainer: .... Date: ....

Workplace address or name of organization:

....

....

....

....

Responsibilities

If you are working in the care profession or just about to start in it, you will have received a job description. This job description will inform you about your roles and responsibilities, what you will be doing and how you should do it. If you need more information on your responsibilities, you could ask colleagues or your manager. You could also read the policies and procedures that are in place and this will help you to meet regulations and legal requirements, reduce risk and follow best practice. When you look through the policies, you are likely to come across a supervision policy. You will read about supervision meetings later on in this workbook.

✍ Write down all the current policies available in your workplace. If you have just started work, what polices have you found out about?

. . . .

. . . .

. . . .

. . . .

Being responsible also means being accountable for your practice. Please write below who you are accountable to and why.

✍ I am accountable to:

. . . .

. . . .

. . . .

. . . .

Why:

. . . .

. . . .

. . . .

. . . .

It is important that you know your own responsibilities and those of your employers.

Take a few minutes here to list some of the responsibilities of your employer:

. . . .

. . . .

. . . .

. . . .

It is important that you understand your role; if you are unclear you should discuss it with your supervisor or manager. If it is unclear, you will not know the knowledge and skills you need and this will prevent you from developing and doing a good job.

Other areas that could affect your performance include the following:

- not having access to care or support plans, so you do not know the specific and individual care and support to give

- not having good role models

- not having support to learn new skills

- not being given money to attend training

- being sent on a standard training course when you need something more specific

- not having regular supervision meetings and appraisals.

✍ Look at your job description and list some of the responsibilities you have:

. . . .

. . . .

. . . .

. . . .

As a social care worker you have a responsibility to support people by providing the very best support and care. You can only do this by:

- thinking about what you are doing, how you are doing it, evaluating it and then doing it a different way if it needs to be done better (this is called 'reflection' and is covered in more depth later on)

- receiving training, including specific training if applicable to your workplace

- looking at the care standards that are applicable to your service

- discussing aspects of your work (this will be covered later on this workbook)

- reading and following polices and procedures.

Following policies and procedures is important as it enables you to follow good practice, reduces risks, ensures consistency and meets legal requirements.

✍ Please ask your manager what guidance your organization has on staff development and write it here:

. . . .

. . . .

. . . .

. . . .

Part of what your manager should have told you will be on meeting the following CQC requirements:

- 50 per cent of staff required to have an NVQ

- managers to have NVQ qualifications

- new staff to complete the:

  - Common Induction Standards or

  - Learning Disability Qualification Induction Award (if supporting people with learning disabilities).

Your manager may also have told you about your responsibilities to:

- identify development and training needs

- attend training courses if applicable and when required

- use your initiative on keeping up to date on new developments; this can be achieved by:

  - searching the web

  - reading professional journals

  - watching documentaries on TV

  - attending conferences

  - linking your responsibilities to discussing and monitoring them as part of supervision which is covered later in this workbook.

Values and Beliefs

As a social care worker you will work with and promote a set of values: respect, privacy, empowerment, inclusion, individuality, independence, dignity, rights, equal opportunities, partnership and choice.

You will have received training in these values when you started your career in care. More information can be found in the GSCC *Code of Practice* (GSCC 2002) and the National Minimum Standards (Department of Health 2000).

We think about the past, present and future; our past has an influence on who we are today and we may often refer back to it. For example, I overheard a conversation where a daughter was asking her mother if she could have a computer so she could email her friends. Her mother said that she could not have one and that it wouldn't do her any harm to walk round to her friends or write a letter as she did when she was her age.

We may have similar traits to other people and do similar things, but we are all individuals with our own values, beliefs and preferences. You will need to be aware that the people you support and the people you work with also have their own values, beliefs and preferences and this makes us all unique.

Case study: one of the people you support, who is 65 years of age, likes to have a bath every other day and on these days he will change his clothes. One of your colleagues has tried to encourage him to change his clothes daily but he says that he does not want to; he has always bathed and changed his clothes every other day. Your colleague is frustrated and believes that people should bathe or shower every day. What are your thoughts on this?

. . . .

. . . .

. . . .

. . . .

Value = this is what really matters to us

For example, some value living near to the shops so they can keep their independence and walk there.

Belief = this is what we believe to be true

For example, a jury in court will all hear the same information but some will believe the person is guilty, others will believe that the person is innocent.

WHERE DO VALUES AND BELIEFS COME FROM?

We get our values and beliefs from:

- growing up with family and friends and being aware of their values and beliefs

- media

- religion

- school

- colleagues at work.

People who are older than you will have grown up with different life experiences, as we saw with the conversation between the mother and her daughter who wanted a computer to email her friends.

Two more examples of this are:

- In Western society during the twentieth century, many men have grown up having different experiences than women. For example, your father or grandfather may have grown up with the belief that the man goes out to work to earn money to support the family while the woman stays at home looking after the children, cooking meals and cleaning the house.

- Some people think that couples have to get married; others believe it is OK to live together.

✍ As we have seen, our past has an influence on who we are today. Think of two things that happened in your past which have influenced you and write them here:

1. . . . .

. . . .

. . . .

. . . .

2. . . . .

. . . .

. . . .

. . . .

People's values and beliefs are different. You are not entitled to judge another person's values or beliefs in a professional context unless his values or beliefs break professional guidelines. If they do, you will need to report it, following your workplace policy on abuse and/or guidance from the workbook *Safeguarding Adults*.

Everyone is different and sees life in different ways. As a social care worker, you need to accept that there are differences and work with them. For example, perhaps you always put the milk in the cup before pouring the tea; your colleague pours the tea and then adds the milk.

✍ Please answer the following two exercises.

A service user would like support to go to a mosque for the first time but you are not a Muslim. Your manager had rostered another staff member on duty to go, but he has gone sick and you are the only one who is available to go with him. Your manager advises that you ring the mosque in advance and ask what you should both wear.

Do you ring ahead and find out more details?   Yes/No

If you have answered 'No', please explain your answer:

. . . .

. . . .

Do you go to the mosque?   Yes/No

What are the consequences if you do not support the service user to go to the mosque?

For you:. . . . .

. . . .

. . . .

. . . .

For the service user:. . . . .

. . . .

. . . .

Think of another way the service user could follow his faith and go to the mosque and write your answer here:

. . . .

. . . .

. . . .

. . . .

You are on shift and you see in the diary that you are rostered to take a service user swimming tomorrow evening. The service user is the same sex as you and goes every Wednesday evening at the local sports centre. The service user has been doing this for a couple of months now and is beginning to get to know some people who go at the same time. You do not want to go swimming because it will rub off your fake tan, spoil your make-up or ruin your hairstyle which took you ages to do.

Do you go swimming?   Yes/No

What are the consequences if you do not support the service user to go swimming?

For you:. . . . .

. . . .

. . . .

. . . .

For the service user:. . . . .

. . . .

. . . .

Think of another way the service user could go swimming on Wednesday evenings and write your answer here:

. . . .

. . . .

. . . .

. . . .

Please discuss your answers with your manager. It is more than likely that you should support both service users in their chosen activities as you are paid to support the service users in whatever they choose to do.

Having said this, there are other ways that the people you support can follow their beliefs and activities without staff being present, either the whole time or some of the time. By discussing your answers to the above questions with your manager, you will both be able to explore these issues further.

Outside of work you can express your values and beliefs to friends and family and act in accordance with them, as long as they or you do not hurt anyone. At work you must respect each individual and provide the same level of care and support to service users who share your values and those who do not. If you do not, you will not be working within the standards of the General Social Care Council.

The General Social Care Council has devised a set of standards that you as a social care worker should work within. These standards contain good practice and professional conduct requirements. There are six standards and the headings of each standard are listed below. You can find out the contents of each standard by obtaining a copy of the *Codes of Practice* from your manager or, if you are recently in post, then you should have received a copy of the booklet in your induction pack. Alternatively you can access a copy on the GSCC website (www.gscc.org.uk).

As a social care worker you must:

1. Protect the rights and promote the interests of service users and carers.

2. Strive to establish and maintain the trust and confidence of service users and carers.

3. Promote the independence of service users while protecting them as far as possible from danger or harm.

4. Respect the rights of service users while seeking to ensure that their behaviour does not harm themselves or other people.

5. Uphold public trust and confidence in social care services.

6. Be accountable for the quality of your work and take responsibility for maintaining and improving your knowledge and skills. (GSCC 2002)

Knowledge and Skills

Throughout your career you will always be learning new skills and knowledge. The people you support have a right to receive a good quality service from trained staff.

You need to take up the opportunities available to update your knowledge and skills which will give you confidence in your practice and meet your objectives and goals.

✎ What would happen if you did not update your knowledge and skills?

. . . .

. . . .

. . . .

. . . .

THE DIFFERENCE BETWEEN KNOWLEDGE AND SKILLS

You may know how to do something and this is called *knowledge*, but you may not necessarily have the ability to put this knowledge into practice and this 'practice' is called a *skill*.

An example could be that you attend a course on epilepsy and hear the knowledge (theory) side of what to do. You may not have had the opportunity to do some role play on how to support a person who is having an epileptic seizure. You return to your workplace with the knowledge of what to do and how to do it but will not yet have the skill to support a person when he/she is having an epileptic seizure.

You will not know that a person is having an epileptic seizure until you see the signs that it is happening. Different feelings and emotions come into play when there is an emergency. If you are in this situation, you could ask your manager if you can do some role play to demonstrate what you have learnt on the course.

Once you have learnt a skill you need to be able to use it regularly otherwise you could forget how to do something or to do it as accurately as is required. If you support people who have well-controlled epilepsy and you therefore do not have the opportunity to use your newly gained knowledge, you could suggest to your manager that you all do role play scenarios in occasional team meetings. This will enable all of you who have received training to keep your knowledge and skills up to date on how to support someone both during and after an epileptic seizure.

 Looking at your job description again, you will see that some of it says:

- know 'how to…' and this means the knowledge that you have

- 'be able to…' and this means the skills that you have or will need to have in order to carry out the task.

TRANSFERRING KNOWLEDGE FROM THE HEAD TO THE HAND

 You may wish to tick in pencil the areas on your job description that you can do (both the knowledge and the skills).

The areas you cannot yet do can be entered into the chart overleaf. You can call this your own Personal Development Plan (PDP) which you can take to your supervision meeting. You will read more about PDPs as you progress through this workbook.

If you are new in post you may wish to discuss this triangle diagram with your manager or supervisor. It will give you a good insight into what you need to achieve and complete within your first six months of being in post.

What I need/want to learn	Why do I need to do it?	How will I do it?

What goals do you want to achieve in the next six months?

Strengths, Weaknesses, Opportunities and Threats (SWOT)

A SWOT analysis is a useful tool in identifying your strengths (what you are good at) and your weaknesses (things that you need to improve on), opportunities (that will enable you to achieve your goals) and threats (that could be an obstacle in achieving).

Strengths (skills and knowledge that you have)	Weaknesses (things that you need to improve on)
Opportunities (opportunities available to promote your development)	Threats (threats to your development, e.g. no money for training, different learning need)

Training

All staff in the care sector need to be trained to a minimum level in the following areas:

- first aid

- food hygiene

- infection control

- safe handling of medication

- fire

- health and safety including assessing risks

- manual handling (if you support people who cannot move); if your role does not involve using hoists etc. then you will still be required to complete training on inanimate loads (e.g. moving or picking up shopping)

- epilepsy (if you support people who have seizures)

- challenging behaviour (if you support people who present challenging behaviour).

Further details of all these areas are given in the *Health and Safety* workbook in this series. If you have not yet attended courses to cover these areas, or your certificate is out of date, then you can list the training you need to do in your own Personal Development Plan.

Another two areas, which are equally important and are a requirement of the Care Quality Commission (CQC), are abuse and communication.

ABUSE

Training on preventing abuse should be given to all members of staff within six months of being in post, along with an annual refresher.

Care staff who are working in domiciliary services must complete training within six months and take a refresher every two years (see *Safeguarding Adults* in this series).

✍ Take some time now and ask yourself these questions:

Have I completed training on preventing abuse?	Yes/No
Do I know what abuse is?	Yes/No
Do I know the symptoms?	Yes/No
Do I know who to report concerns to?	Yes/No

If you have answered 'No' to two or more of these questions, what is this telling you?

It is telling you that you need to know more about abuse. You can enter the details in your Personal Development Plan chart and take it to your next supervision meeting.

While waiting to complete this training, you should read your organizational policy on abuse.

COMMUNICATION

You must be able to communicate with all the people you are supporting.

✍ Do you know how to communicate with every service user? This is a big question as 'communication' is a vital skill.

Think of the people you support in the workplace one at a time and answer the following questions (for confidentiality reasons please do not write the person's name or initials):

Do I have a two-way conversation with him/her?   Yes/No

If you answered 'No' please explain why (e.g. 'The service user cannot talk so we do not have a conversation').

. . . .

. . . .

. . . .

. . . .

Does the person I support do all the talking? Yes/No

If you answered 'No', please explain why (e.g. 'The service user tries to tell me what he needs but I cannot understand what he's trying to tell me').

. . . .

. . . .

. . . .

. . . .

If you have answered 'No' to these questions, what is this telling you? It is telling you that you need to gain some knowledge and skills on how to communicate with the people you support. Have a think now about how you will do this. Remember: to learn something doesn't mean that you have to go on a course. You could for example watch how others communicate with a particular service user, search the web for information or work through another book in this series, *Effective Communication*.

Complete your Personal Development Plan on how you will learn the skills and knowledge needed for you to be able to communicate with the people you support. You could then discuss this in supervision with your supervisor.

Learning

We learn something new every day, sometimes without realizing that it is learning. However, some people say that you need to go on a course to learn.

✍ Think about something you learnt yesterday at work that did not involve going on a training course.

. . . .

. . . .

Here are a few examples:

- A service user tells you she is now going to be a vegetarian.

- Another service user says he wants to stop having toast for breakfast as the crumbs stick in his throat and he wants to have cereal instead.

- After reading an updated care plan, you find that the service user now wishes to have a lie-in on Sunday mornings.

- After reading a risk assessment, you now know how you should support a service user to cross a busy road.

HOW DO YOU LEARN BEST?

Knowing this is crucial. Not everyone stops to think about how they learn best. Attending a training course will meet some people's needs, other people will need different ways to learn. Some examples are given later, under the heading 'Identifying learning styles'.

The time of learning can have an impact on learning, e.g. some people may learn better:

- in the morning

- in the afternoon

- in the evening

- before meals

- after meals

- at night.

Before we look at this further you may like to try this exercise:

 Observe the time you read a newspaper or magazine at home or a policy document at work and if you have absorbed or retained what you had read. If you have not, then the time you read it was not your 'best time' to learn. You may wish to try this exercise a few times to find out which is your best time.

THE PROCESS OF LEARNING

We are not born with learning skills, we have to develop them. The process of learning is shown in the diagram.

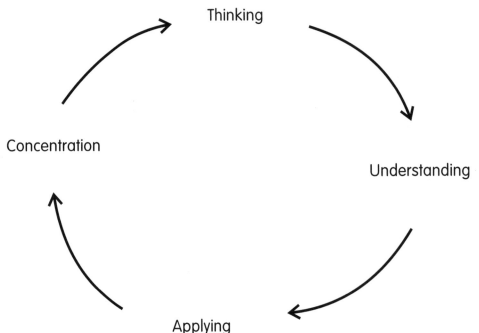

 You have been on a training course where you were taught different ways of communicating with the people you support. When you are next at work, you look forward to using some of the ways to communicate with a service user who has no verbal communication. How would you know if you were communicating in the way that this person preferred?

. . . .

. . . .

. . . .

. . . .

IDENTIFYING LEARNING STYLES

We all learn in different ways, e.g. some people learn by:

- watching others who are more experienced

- reading literature, e.g. journals, articles

- going to the library

- attending training courses

- searching the Internet for information

- having discussions in groups, team meetings, supervision meetings.

It will be beneficial for you to identify your learning style as soon as you can. If you do not do this, it could hinder you reaching your goals. For example, if you learn best by watching others then your manager could arrange for you to shadow another person with those skills, rather than read a book about it.

There are a variety of learning style questionnaires around, on CD-Rom, in books, on websites and so on. Some learning style questionnaires need to be purchased; however, one that is free and can be accessed on the Internet is the VAK (visual, auditory, kinaesthetic) questionnaire.

The VAK questionnaire enables you to assess your preferred learning style by completing a set of questions. The questions are listed a, b, c, and you will be asked to circle the items that are most appropriate to you. At the end you will count how many a's, b's and c's you have scored. It will then tell you if your preferred learning style is:

- *visual*: learns by seeing, e.g. presentations, demonstrations, pictures

- *auditory*: learns by listening

- *kinesthetic*: learns by doing, i.e. hands on experience.

You may have one strong preferred learning style or a mix of all three styles.

Your manager or training manager may have copies of these. Alternatively you can access the VAK questionnaire on the Internet (www.businessballs.com) or by visiting your local library.

DIFFERENT LEARNING NEEDS

If you have a different learning need, e.g. difficulty in reading or writing, you can contact Learndirect (www.learndirect.co.uk) and arrange for a word skills check. In the word skills check, you answer a set of questions on a computer; your answers will be checked against the national standards and will show the areas that you need some support in, e.g. reading or writing.

Different learning needs can include people with dyslexia, people who are deaf, people with English as a second language, people with reading and/or writing difficulties, people who are visually impaired and so on.

You may prefer not to tell your manager or supervisor if you have a different learning need, but if you do not, he/she cannot put things in place to help you.

> A person with a different learning need may need a different type of learning from that of conventionally taught training courses.

Reflective Practice

A good way of learning is to think about what worked well and what has not worked well in the past. It is good practice to look at what you have done and evaluate it as this will enable you to know if what you are doing is the most appropriate way to do something.

Discussion in groups at staff meetings or on training courses can be another way of reflecting: as you discuss the topic you will hear other people's points of view and this will enable you to develop and promote good practice.

✎ Give an example of a training course you attended recently and what you learnt from going on it:

. . . .

. . . .

. . . .

. . . .

Reflective cycle

Graham Gibbs (1988) depicted reflection as a cycle. Something has to occur, then feelings and thoughts come (good and bad) and you evaluate the good and bad things that have happened. The next step is to think about what you have learnt from the occasion. You then look at how you could have done it differently and the final stage of this cycle is to think about what you would do if it happened again.

Description
What happened?

Feelings
*What were you
thinking and feeling?*

Action plan
*If it arose again
what would you do?*

Evaluation
*What was good and bad
about the experience?*

Conclusion
*What could you have
done differently?*

Analysis
*What can you learn from
what has happened?*

(Gibbs 1988)[1]

✎ Please take a few minutes to complete this exercise:

What I did recently at work:

. . . .

. . . .

. . . .

. . . .

. . . .

1   Reproduced with kind permission of Graham Gibbs

What was I thinking and feeling?

. . . .

. . . .

. . . .

. . . .

What was good and bad about the experience?

. . . .

. . . .

. . . .

. . . .

What did I learn from what has happened?

. . . .

. . . .

. . . .

. . . .

What could I have done differently?

. . . .

. . . .

. . . .

. . . .

If it arose again what would I do?

. . . .

. . . .

. . . .

. . . .

Please take this exercise to discuss with your manager or supervisor in your next supervision meeting.

Taking time to review your own work is beneficial and discussing it in supervision is all part of good reflective practice. Your supervisor will want to see that you are taking some responsibility for your own learning and development and this will be one way to show this.

Keeping Up to Date

Part of your responsibility will be to keep yourself up to date on:

- best practice
- lessons learned from poor practice
- legislation and new ways of working.

BEST PRACTICE

'Best practice' is an idea that is made into a standard that should be followed to achieve an outcome in the most effective way, for example meeting an individual's needs. Several reports on good practice that you may wish to read are available at www.valuingpeople.gov.uk/dynamic/valuingpeople2.jsp

You may also like to look at the following:

- Good practice guidance on working with parents with a learning disability: the Department of Health and the Department for Education and Science have put together a good practice guidance on how adult and children's services should work together to improve support to parents with a learning disability and their children.

- Oral health: the Department of Health have brought out a good practice guide for improving the oral health of disabled children and adults. To see this guide, please go to: www.dh.gov/en/Aboutus/Chiefprofessionalofficers/Chiefdentalofficer /DH_4138822.

- Services for People with Learning Disabilities and Challenging Behaviour or Mental Health Needs: this report looks at people with difficult and challenging behaviour and the services that support them in their everyday lives.

LESSONS LEARNED FROM POOR PRACTICE

You may wish to read these reports on investigations into poor practice.

Sutton and Merton Primary Care Trust: In 2006 the Healthcare Commission investigated the service provided for people with a learning disability at Sutton and Merton Primary Care Trust, following a request from the chief executive of the Primary Care Trust (PCT). This request was for an investigation into allegations of physical and sexual abuse. You can find out more by going onto the Internet and go to the Voice UK website (www.voiceuk.org.uk/ sutton.htm).

Harold Shipman: Harold Shipman was a general practitioner who was convicted of murdering 15 of his patients in January 2000. It was poor practice that led to his crimes going unnoticed for so long. You can find out more by going onto the Internet at www.the-shipman-inquiry.org.uk/reports.asp

Staffordshire Council: A report on Staffordshire Council's controversial support of 'pindown', a method of restraining 'intractable' children in care by using techniques akin to solitary confinement. See http://ftvdb.bfi.org.uk/ sift/title/635467

Victoria Climbié: Victoria Climbié died in hospital on 25 February 2000 with 128 injuries to her body. A public inquiry was set up after the murder conviction of her carers Marie-Therese Kouao and Carl Manning, in January 2001. The Report of the Victoria Climbié Inquiry by Lord Laming was published on 28 January 2003 following three inquiries using powers under the Children Act 1989, NHS Act 1977 and Police Act 1996. See https://www.rcgp.org.uk/ pdf/ISS_SUMM03_02.pdf

Baby P: Town halls no longer meeting standards in safeguarding children include Haringey Council, where Baby P was allowed to die after suffering months of abuse, despite being on an at-risk register and having been seen 78 times by social workers and doctors. See www.harringey.gov.uk/index/ news_and_events/latest_news/childa.htm

✐ Ask your manager for a copy of the latest CQC inspection report for your workplace. If you are unable to get a copy, you can go onto the CQC website (www.cqc.org.uk) and access a copy. After reading it please specify which parts of it have influenced you and explain why:

. . . .

. . . .

. . . .

. . . .

LEGISLATION AND NEW WAYS OF WORKING

Legislation changes from time to time and when it does it can affect the way you work, so you have to work in a different way. The following websites will have up-to-date information on new legislation:

Department of Health (www.dh.gov.uk): provides health and social care policy, guidance and publications for NHS and social care professionals.

Care Quality Commission (www.cqc.org.uk): inspect and report on care services and councils; are independent but set up by the government to improve on social care and stamp out bad practice.

Department for Children, Schools and Families (www.dcsf.gov.uk): looks after the wellbeing of children and young people in terms of health, safety, education and helping them stay on track.

Support and Feedback

You will receive feedback in a supportive way from your supervisor in your supervision meetings and this feedback should be clear, specific, honest and non-judgemental. You cannot do a good job if you do not receive feedback! The feedback can be positive and constructive, informing you of the things you have done well and the areas you need to improve on. You should not feel bad about receiving constructive feedback; this is given to you so you know what you have to improve on. Your supervisor will put things in place to help you achieve this.

Feedback can also be given at other times and in different formats, e.g. verbally, in the communication or handover book, in a letter etc. You need to receive feedback on how you are doing as it is difficult to analyse yourself. You need to ask yourself how objective you can be.

> Feedback encourages development. Positive and constructive feedback boosts self-esteem, self-worth and motivation.

You can obtain feedback in other ways and here are a few examples:

- If you are new, you may have a 'buddy' assigned to you. He/she can help you settle in and give you feedback.

- If there are senior staff on shift, they will be supporting you by showing you how to do tasks and giving you feedback.

- Ask the people you support if you are supporting them in the way they wish you to. It will depend on the individual as to how you ask the question. During the support you are providing, you could say 'Is this OK?' and after the support you could say something like 'Was that OK, did you like the way I washed your hair?' etc.

- You could watch the individual's body language; it can tell you so much.

Body language and forms of communication are covered in the workbook *Effective Communication*.

There will be times when you are with others who can also give you feedback on what you are doing. It does not have to be long winded: sometimes a smile and 'thank you' from someone is good feedback. Others who can give you feedback can be:

- other professionals, e.g. district nurses, social workers

- service users' families

- visitors.

By being approachable, people will give you feedback and share information with you on what you need to know to support a service user. In this way you are developing your knowledge.

Feedback is not just a one-way process; you can also give feedback to others.

Supervision

WHAT IS SUPERVISION?

Supervision is 'to direct or oversee the performance or operation of' (Collins Dictionary, 1987). This is a good definition, as you will need to be directed and have your performance overseen very frequently in the early days of employment and then when required to meet various standards.

In the care sector 'supervision meetings' are linked to the annual appraisal, where goals are set for the following year. The appraisal evaluates the worker's progress over a 12-month period and the supervision meetings monitor the working towards and completion of the goals. These goals are broken down into objectives and entered onto a Personal Development Plan and you can read more about this on p.47.

Supervision meetings are regular planned meetings between a care worker and someone in a higher position; this can be the manager or someone the manager delegates this to, e.g. senior carer, assistant or deputy manager.

The supervision meetings will identify organizational, professional and personal objectives and can include the needs of the following:

- service users

- organization

- supervisee

- supervisor.

These supervision meetings are facilitated by a supervisor.

> Supervision is a tool for the development of performance and a key part of quality assurance and providing a skilled and professional workforce.

WHO IS A SUPERVISOR AND WHAT IS HIS ROLE?

A supervisor is a senior member of staff who holds the position of manager, deputy or senior. Supervision meetings are facilitated by a senior staff member who has undergone training to become a 'supervisor' with responsibilities to facilitate supervision meetings and support the care worker to develop and plan his objectives.

An employee's performance is discussed at every supervision meeting. A record, written by the supervisor, is called the 'supervision minutes'. The minutes will be signed and dated by the supervisor and supervisee and both will keep a copy of the minutes.

If you are new to the role, you will have these supervision meetings and you will also have a review meeting which will consider how you are progressing in your new position. Some organizations have a three-month review with another review at the end of the employee's probationary period (which can be six months).

There are various names for supervision meetings, e.g. 'one-to-one sessions' and 'support sessions'.

THE PURPOSE AND IMPORTANCE OF SUPERVISION

The Care Quality Commission (CQC) has provided standards that need to be met in order to provide a safe environment for vulnerable people. Some of these standards include the need for supervision meetings.

There are standards for various care groups, e.g. children, younger adults, older people. For example, two CQC standards are Care Homes for Adults Standard 36 (Department of Health 2003) and Domiciliary Care Standard 21 (Department of Health 2000).

Care Homes for Adults Standard 36 (36.4)

> Staff have regular, recorded supervision meetings at least six times a year with their senior/manager in addition to regular contact on day to day practice (fortnightly where there is no regular contact; pro-rata for part-time staff).

Domiciliary Care Standard 21 (21.1 and 21.2)

> All care and support staff receive regular supervision and have their standard of practice appraised annually.

> All staff meet formally on a one to one basis with their line manager to discuss their work at least 3 monthly and written records kept on the content and outcome of each meeting. (See Standard 27.3)

There are other standards relevant to your work as an employee in the care sector, e.g. the General Social Care Council Standard 6:

as a social care worker, they must be accountable for the quality of their work and take responsibility for maintaining and improving their knowledge and skills. (GSCC 2002)

THE BENEFITS OF SUPERVISION MEETINGS

Supervision meetings are regular planned events on a one-on-one basis and the only thing that should prevent them from happening is an emergency!

Supervision provides a safe environment in that these sessions are confidential and most of the time things discussed in the supervision meeting stay in the meeting. However, your written supervision minutes may need to be passed on if there is an investigation, or if your supervisor's manager wishes to see them to ensure that you are being supervised correctly or if the Care Quality Commission wishes to see them as part of its auditing.

It gives time to discuss your development and focuses on you. It also clarifies your roles and the responsibilities you have. You will be supported and informed of what you need to achieve and how to achieve it. It will praise you for things you have done well and will offer advice on how to do other things better, i.e. it will regularly evaluate your progress.

Problems and stress at work can be discussed and it is important that you do this because your supervisor needs to know how you are feeling and by telling him/her the problems you are experiencing at work, your supervisor can help in deciding what can be done to reduce your stress levels. It is said that a little stress is good for the body but too much stress could have an effect on the service you provide to the people you support and your colleagues, and cause ill health for yourself.

Your supervisor can pass information from management to you and the organization will be able to provide a better service delivery through you. This means that the people you support will receive a better level of support and quality of life.

Training needs are identified. Prior to putting you forward for any training, you and your supervisor will discuss the training you require and the contents of a training course to see if it meets your need. Following the training, you will both discuss in the next supervision meeting if it has met your need and how you will introduce your newly gained knowledge into the workplace.

GETTING THE MOST FROM YOUR SUPERVISION MEETINGS

Your supervisor should tell you in advance of when you will be having a supervision meeting and where it will be held.

Before the supervision meeting

- Have a look at the minutes of your last supervision. Is there anything that needs to be brought forward to your next supervision?

- Make a list of things you would like to discuss and get advice on.

Be prepared, take with you:

- Pen and paper.

- Copy of last supervision minutes.

- List of things you wish to discuss. Your supervisor will have his or her list too: at the beginning of the meeting you can discuss your individual lists together and put them into one list which your supervisor can follow during the meeting.

- A glass of water. You could ask your supervisor if he would like one too.

During the supervision meeting

- discuss action points from your last supervision

- discuss areas of work

- identify training needs

- ask questions if you are unsure of anything

- don't spend longer than is needed on each topic

- try to keep to the subject you are talking about

- set goals

- remember it is *your* supervision, make the most of it

- set a date for the next supervision that is convenient to you both.

After the supervision meeting

- implement any changes in work practice

- start working towards achieving the goals.

Finally, enjoy your supervision meeting; they are great supportive sessions which if used positively can enhance your career!

CONTRACTS

Your supervisor will discuss a supervision contract with you in your first supervision session. This sets out how your supervision will be run, where the confidential minutes of the meetings will be kept and so on.

Probation reviews can be completed during supervision meetings. However some managers may prefer for a probation review to be in a meeting by itself. Annually you will receive an appraisal which can be done by the supervisor and/or manager. Appraisals are discussed in a separate section (see p.52).

If you are new in post, please ask your manager:

When will I have a supervision meeting? . . . .

. . . .

Who will it be with?. . . . .

. . . .

PERSONAL DEVELOPMENT PLAN

Personal Development Plans (PDPs) are important working documents and will identify your training and development needs. They enable you and your supervisor to set objectives and goals and explore the best methods to achieve them. Your supervisor will support you with these and this is a good way of tracking your progress.

Your Personal Development Plan is unique to you. It may have some similar goals to another colleague on it, e.g. if you both need to know how to support a service user with road skills then both of your PDPs will have this as an objective.

It should be used and not put in a filing cabinet and never seen again. Do you remember earlier on in this workbook you were completing your own Personal Development Plan? A plan that your supervisor has may contain a few more columns and an example of what it could look like is on the next page.

What I need/want to learn	Why do I need to do it?	How will I do it?	When will I do it?	Review date

You can devise the PDP with your supervisor, have dates to achieve objectives and goals and review it regularly.

The PDP will have a front page and this page can contain the following entries.

Name:. . . . .

Name of workplace:. . . . .

Name of supervisor:. . . . .

Goals:. . . . .

. . . .

. . . .

. . . .

. . . .

. . . .

. . . .

. . . .

. . . .

. . . .

Signed by staff member: . . . . Date: . . . .

Signed by supervisor:. . . . . Date: . . . .

Date to be reviewed: . . . .

GET SMART!

A good way of setting out the process or activity to reach a goal is to use 'SMART':

- **S**pecific

- **M**easurable

- **A**chievable

- **R**ealistic and relevant

- **T**ime bound.

An example of using SMART to set and measure an objective is shown in the table.

Specific	Measurable	Achievable	Realistic and relevant	Time bound
The care worker will learn BSL sign language to enable him to communicate with service user X	Attend training course	Yes	Yes	End of December 2009

> SMART is setting up signposts to enable the supervisee to achieve his goals.

Many organizations have their own design of a Personal Development Plan. When breaking down the goals into objectives and entering them onto a PDP, the SMART format can be used.

✍ Give two examples of how you have used your supervision as a way of improving your work practice.

1. . . . .

. . . .

. . . .

. . . .

2. . . . .

. . . .

. . . .

. . . .

Please remember that while supervision is important in helping towards good practice, there are other equally important ways to improve your practice, e.g. discussions with colleagues, team meetings, attending courses and reading.

Appraisal

WHAT IS AN APPRAISAL?

An appraisal is a planned meeting between the person who holds responsibility for the employee and the employer. This could be a manager, deputy or senior. Appraisals are held annually.

SELF-APPRAISAL FORM

Prior to your appraisal you will be asked to complete a self-appraisal form. This form may ask questions such as:

- Which aspects of your job have you done well?

- Why do you think this?

- Which aspects of your job have you had difficulty with?

- Why do you think this?

When completing this it will give you an opportunity to reflect on what you have done well during the past year and areas that could be improved on. It allows you to evaluate your own practice. Your supervisor will also complete an appraisal form where he/she will be evaluating your practice. During your appraisal meeting you will both discuss what is written on your forms and agree some objectives for you to achieve during the next year to improve and enhance your development.

PURPOSE OF AN APPRAISAL

The purpose of an appraisal is to review, discuss and evaluate the goals that were set for the employee from the previous year and set new ones for the following year. The appraisal is an ongoing part of supervision, because in supervision sessions you will be discussing and being supported by your supervisor to reach the goals set from the appraisal. You and your supervisor will agree the objectives.

WHAT IS A GOAL?

A goal is a set of objectives. The objectives are small steps that you are going to work towards in order to reach the goals you have set. You will have read about this in the section on Supervision.

✍ Now that you have reached the end of this workbook you might wish to
write down a list of some of the different ways you could improve your
practice.

. . . .

. . . .

. . . .

. . . .

Reflecting on the list you have made, what one thing will you do differently in
the future in your workplace?

. . . .

. . . .

Self-Assessment Tool

✎ I now know:

What my responsibilities are	Yes/No
The process of learning	Yes/No
How to find my learning style	Yes/No
How to reflect on my practice	Yes/No
Keeping up to date	Yes/No
What feedback is and how to get it	Yes/No
What a supervision meeting is and its benefits	Yes/No
The role of a supervisor	Yes/No
What a supervision contract is	Yes/No
What a Personal Development Plan is	Yes/No
What an appraisal is	Yes/No

Signature of learner . . . . Date . . . .

Signature of supervisor . . . . Date . . . .

When you have completed this self-assessment tool, please do not worry if you have answered 'No' as you can go back and read the relevant sections again.

Certificate

. . . .

Name of company

THIS IS TO CERTIFY THAT

. . . .

Name of learner

Has completed training on

Reflecting On and Developing Your Practice

ON

. . . .

Date

Name of Manager/Trainer. . . . .

Signature of Manager/Trainer. . . . .

Name of workplace/training venue . . . .

Date . . . .

This is to be written on the back of the certificate:

This training has covered:

- Responsibilities
- Values and beliefs
- Knowledge and skills
- Strengths, Weaknesses, Opportunities and Threats (SWOT)
- Training
- Learning skills
- The process of learning
- Learning styles
- Different learning needs
- Reflective practice
- Keeping up to date
- Support and feedback
- Supervision
- Contracts
- Personal Development Plan
- Appraisal

Knowledge Specification Chart

WHERE TO FIND THE KNOWLEDGE SPECIFICATION (KS) FOR NVQ UNIT 33

KS		Pages
1	Legal and organizational requirements on equality, diversity, discrimination and rights when working with individuals and others to improve your knowledge and practice.	12, 16, 27, 41, 43, 46
2	Dilemmas and conflicts that you may face in your practice.	13, 16
3	Codes of practice and conduct; standards and guidance relevant to your own and others' roles, responsibilities, accountability and duties about personal and professional development.	9, 10, 12, 14, 15, 16, 21, 27, 30, 43
4	Current local, UK and European legislation, and organizational requirements, procedures and practices for accessing training and undertaking personal and professional development activities.	39
5	The purpose of, and arrangements for, your supervision and appraisal.	43
6	How and where to access information and support on knowledge and best practice relevant to your area of work, the individuals and key people with whom you work and the skills and knowledge you need to practise effectively.	39, 40
7	Principles underpinning personal and professional development and reflective practice.	16, 30, 34
8	How to work in partnership with individuals, key people and others to enable you to develop and enhance your knowledge and practice.	41, 43

9	Development opportunities that can enhance your practice.	14, 25, 26, 32, 43
10	Lessons learned from inquiries into serious failure of health and social care practice, and from successful interventions.	38
11	Approaches to learning that will allow you to transfer your knowledge and skills to new and unfamiliar contexts.	16, 26, 27, 30, 34, 39, 41, 43

Legislation and Useful Websites

LEGISLATION THAT COULD BE APPLICABLE TO THE PEOPLE YOU SUPPORT

Care Standards Act 2000

The Care Standards Act 2000 (CSA) provides for the administration of a variety of care institutions, including children's homes, independent hospitals, nursing homes and residential care homes.

Data Protection Act 1998

This Act protects the rights of the individual on information that is obtained, stored, processed or supplied and applies to both computerized and paper records and requires that appropriate security measures are in place.

Human Rights Act 2000

This Act promotes the fundamental rights and freedoms contained in the European Convention on Human Rights.

Mental Capacity Act 2005

This Act provides a clearer legal framework for people who lack capacity and sets out key principles and safeguards. It also includes the 'Deprivation of liberty safeguards' which aims to provide legal protection for vulnerable people who are deprived of their liberty other than under the Mental Health Act 1983. It is planned to come into effect in April 2009.

Mental Health Act 1983

This Act regulates the treatment of mentally ill people.

NHS and Community Care Act 1990

This Act helps people live safely in the community.

Safeguarding Vulnerable Groups Act 2006

This aim of this Act is to strengthen current safeguarding arrangements and prevent unsuitable people from working with children and adults who are vulnerable. It will change the way vetting happens and will be introduced gradually from autumn 2008.

Sexual Offences Act 2003

This Act makes new provision about sexual offences, their prevention and the protection of children from harm and sexual acts.

USEFUL WEBSITES

All the following websites were accessed on 15 November 2008.

Care Quality Commission

www.cqc.org.uk

CQC inspect and report on care services and councils and are independent but set up by government to improve social care and stamp out bad practice.

Department of Health

www.dh.gov.uk

Providing health and social care policy, guidance and publications for NHS and social care professionals.

General Social Care Council

www.gscc.org.uk

Sets standards of conduct and practice for social care workers and their employers in England.

Learndirect

www.learndirect.co.uk

Courses are flexible and you can do many of the courses at your local centre or from home or work if you have access to the Internet. Courses are broken down into bite-sized chunks, so you can learn at your own pace whenever and wherever suits you.

Learning and Skills Council

www.lsc.gov.uk

The Learning and Skills Council exists to make England better skilled and more competitive.

Skills for Care

www.skillsforcare.org.uk

Skills for Care is the employer-led authority on the training standards and development needs of nearly one million social care staff in England providing over £25 million in funding to support improved training and qualifications for managers and staff.

Skills for Health

www.skillsforhealth.org.uk

Skills for Health is the Sector Skills Council (SSC) for the UK health sector. They help the whole sector develop solutions that deliver a skilled and flexible UK workforce in order to improve health and healthcare.

Valuing People

www.valuingpeople.gov.uk

Valuing People is the government's plan for making the lives of people with learning disabilities and their families better.

Voice UK

www.voiceuk.org.uk

Voice UK is a national charity supporting people with learning disabilities and other vulnerable people who have experienced crime or abuse.

References and Further Reading

REFERENCES

Department of Health (2000) *Domiciliary Care: National Minimum Standards* (Commission for Social Care Inspection Communication Standard). London: Stationery Office. Available at www.dh.gov.uk/prod_consum_dh/groups/dh_digitalassets/@dh/@en/documents/digi talasset/dh_4018671.pdf, accessed on 19 October 2008.

Department of Health (2003) *Care Homes for Adults (18–65)* (Commission for Social Care Inspection Communication Standard). London: Stationery Office. Available at www.csci.org.uk/professional/care_providers/all_services/national_minimum_standards. aspx, accessed on 19 October 2008.

General Social Care Council (GSCC) (2002) *Codes of Practice*. London: GSCC. Available at www.gscc.org.uk, accessed on 19 October 2008.

Gibbs, G. (1988) *Learning by Doing: A Guide to Teaching and Learning Methods*. London: Further Education Unit. Gibbs' reflective cycle is available at www.health.uce.ac.uk/dpl/nursing/Placement%20Support/Model%20of%Reflection.htm, accessed on 15 November 2008.

FURTHER READING

Alsop, A. (2000) *Continuing Professional Development: A Guide for Therapists*. Oxford: Blackwell Science.

Parham, D. (1987) 'Towards professionalism: the reflective therapist.' *American Journal of Occupational Therapy 41*, 9, 555–561.

Schon, D. (1991) *The Reflective Practitioner. How Professionals Think in Action*. San Francisco, CA: Jossey-Bass.